I0213643

Explain to Me Again How This World Began

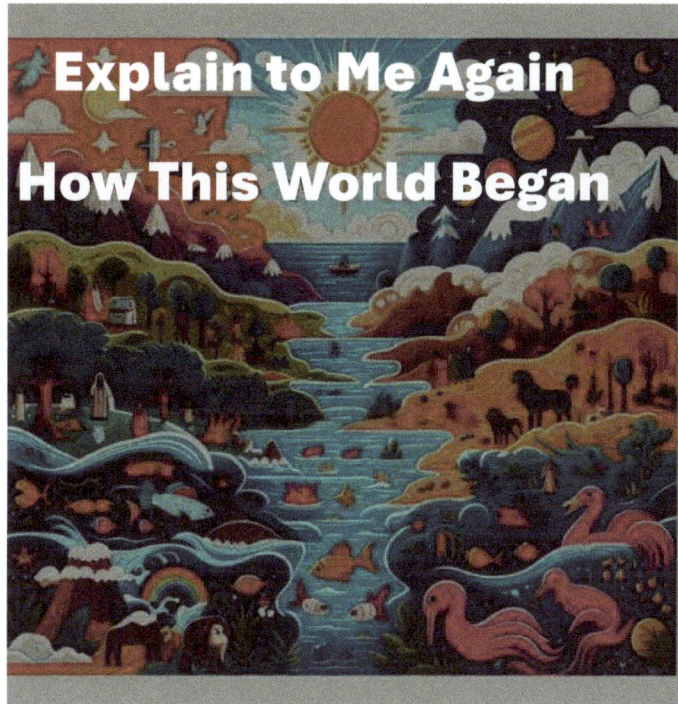

Gwendolyn L. Smith

Copyright @ 2024 Gwendolyn L. Smith

All rights reserved. No part of this publication may be reproduced, distributed, or transmitted without the prior written permission from the copyright holder.

ISBN 979-8-218-74554-7

Explain to Me Again
How This World Began

In the Beginning

Day One

As the sun sets, the sky looks as though someone gracefully colored it pink, red, blue, and yellow, as it slowly fades away for the night to appear. A warm and gentle breeze softly blows causing the leaves on the trees to sway back and forth. Darkness comes forth, yet there is light from the moon and the stars that shine bright.

Listen! Do you hear anything? All is quiet, except the sound of crickets

Do you ever wonder who made the sun and the moon, or how the stars stay up in the sky, or how many stars there are? No one knows but God. It tells us in the Bible, "In the beginning, God created the sky and the earth."

¹In the beginning God created the sky and the earth. ² The earth was empty and had no form. Darkness covered the ocean, and God's Spirit was moving over the water.

[Genesis 1:1-2 International Children's Bible (ICB)]

Before God created the Sky and the Earth there was no life.

Follow along and find out more of how this World began.

³Then God said, "Let there be light!"

And there was light. ⁴God saw the light was good. So he
divided the light from the darkness. ⁵God named the light
"day" and the darkness "night." Evening passed and morning
came. This was the first day. (Genesis 1:3–5 ICB)

How many days do you think it took God to create the World? Five days, six days, or seven days?

Let's find out.

You will be AMAZED!

Day Two

⁶ Then God said, "Let there be something to divide the water in two!" ⁷ So God made the air to divide the water in two. Some of the water was above the air, and some of the water was below it. ⁸ God named the air "sky." Evening passed, and morning came. This was the second day. (Genesis 1:6–8 ICB)

Day Two is Done!

This is so exciting and
so much fun!

Day Three

⁹ Then God said, "Let the water under the sky be gathered together so the dry land will appear." And it happened. ¹⁰ God named the dry land "earth." He named the water that was gathered together "seas." God saw that this was good.

¹¹ Then God said, "Let the earth produce plants. Some plants will make grain for seeds. Others will make fruit with seeds in it. Every seed will produce more of its own kind of plant." And it happened. ¹² The earth produced plants. Some plants had grain for seeds. The trees made fruit with seeds in it. Each seed grew its own kind of plant. God saw that all this was good. ¹³ Evening passed, and morning came. This was the third day. (Genesis 1:9–13 ICB)

We all know there are rivers and seas . . . Achoo, Bless you!
The breeze from the Seas can be quite chilly, sorry it made
you sneeze. The Oceans and Seas all have a name, but as you
see, none are the same.

Seas ➡️

Mediterranean Sea   The Caspian Sea
The Adriatic Sea   The Arabian Sea
The Persian Gulf   The Black Sea
The Red Sea

Oceans ➡️

The Pacific Ocean   The Atlantic Ocean
The Indian Ocean   The Southern Ocean
The Arctic Ocean

Fact: Rivers provide clean water for animals and people. It is a smaller body of water that runs downhill into an ocean or sea. The clean water from the river helps reduce the salt in the oceans so it will not become too salty

Ah! Fruit! Fruit is so good *and* is good for your body. Not all the fruit will be named, I know you care, here are few unique fruits that we can share. You may live in Ecuador and eat a Naranjilla tropical fruit.

(Pronounced: närən'hēlyə) The outside looks like an orange, the pulp on the inside is green with a tangy taste — almost like a lemon — But taste good — Kinda!

Perhaps you live in Thailand and eat a tropical mangosteen fruit. It can take up to ten to twenty years for the fruit to ripen. That's a long time.

It looks like a plum, but on the inside, it has a white filling. The taste is a mixture of banana, peach, and lychee. This fruit is called the Queen of Fruit in Southeast Asia. WHAT? It is because it has a sweet and sour taste combined!

Are you from the Philippines? If you are, there is a delicious fruit in your country called The Durian fruit.

It has a prickly hard outer shell, and when sliced open, it has a strong odor, with a creamy custard taste that is so good it melts in your mouth like ice cream — with flavors of caramel, vanilla, banana, and cheese all wrapped up in one.

Maybe you live in America and eat fruit called a Pawpaw. In the state of Ohio, there are many Pawpaw trees. How does it taste? Well, there is banana flavor in it, kiwi flavor in it, and mango flavor in it all mixed together. Whoa, that looks like a giant jumping bean!

How many days have we done so far? Yes three. I'm sure there is more, let's see . . .

☀️ 🌙 Day Four

¹⁴ Then God said, "Let there be lights in the sky to separate day from night. These lights will be used for signs, seasons, days and years. ¹⁵ They will be in the sky to give light to the earth." And it happened. ¹⁶ So God made the two large lights. He made the brighter light to rule the day. He made the smaller light to rule the night. He also made the stars. ¹⁷ God put all these in the sky to shine on the earth. ¹⁸ They are to rule over the day and over the night. He put them there to separate the light from the darkness. God saw that all these things were good. ¹⁹ Evening passed, and morning came. This was the fourth day. (Genesis 1:14–19 ICB)

Aww! Now we know how God put the Sun, the Moon, and the stars in the sky. When the night is clear and the moon shines bright, it is tempting to count how many stars there are. Try if you will but remember that the sky is seen all over the world. There is not a number anyone knows that is exact. However, God knows all things, and that is a fact.

Day Five 🐠

²⁰ Then God said, "Let the water be filled with living things. And let birds fly in the air above the earth." ²¹ So God created the large sea animals. He created every living thing that moves in the sea. The sea is filled with these living things, Each one produces more of its own kind. God also made every bird that flies. And each bird produces more of its own kind. God saw that this was good. ²² God blessed them and said, "Have many young ones and grow in number. Fill the water of the seas, and let the birds grow in number on the earth." ²³ Evening passed, and morning came. This was the fifth day. (Genesis 1:20–23 ICB)

The oceans and seas are very powerful. During a storm the waves can reach so high, almost to the sky, that when they come crashing down, they can destroy a ship. Besides that, these massive oceans and seas are filled with colorful, playful sea life of every shape and size, along with the breathtaking coral reefs. Did you see the Blue Whale? He said "Hi."

Birds help us in the World grow more trees, plants, and fruit. How, you ask? They eat plants and fruit with seeds in them. Well, not all birds, some birds eat meat. But the birds that do eat fruit and plants with seeds in them fly to many places and release the seeds in their droppings. Plop! The droppings fall to the ground, and then seeds will grow into another tree, or more beautiful flowers, or more fruit trees.

Is this a real bird? Of course it is. It is a Gouldian finch. (Pronounced like the word golden) You can only see them in Australia. You might have to become a World traveler to see more fascinating birds — That would be AWESOME!

Day Six

²⁴ Then God said, "Let the earth be filled with animals. And let each produce more of its own kind. Let there be tame animals and small crawling animals and wild animals. And let each produce more of its kind." And it happened.

²⁵ So God made the wild animals, the tame animals and all the small crawling animals to produce more of their own kind. God saw that this was good.

²⁶ Then God said, "Let us make human beings in our image and likeness. And let them rule over the fish in the sea and the birds in the sky. Let them rule over the tame animals, over all the earth and over all the small crawling animals on the earth." ²⁷ So God created human beings in his image. In the image of God he created them. He created them male and female. ²⁸ God blessed them and said, "Have many children and grow in number. Fill the earth and be its master. Rule over the fish in the sea and over the birds in the sky. Rule over every living thing that moves on the earth."

²⁹ God said, "Look, I have given you all the plants that have grain for seeds. And I have given you all the trees whose fruits have seeds in them. They will be food for you. ³⁰ I have given all the green plants to all the animals to eat. They will be food for every wild animal, every bird of the air and every small crawling animal." And it happened. ³¹ God looked at everything he had made, and it was very good. Evening passed, and morning came. This was the sixth day. (Genesis 1:24–31 ICB)

6 days are done. Let's review . . .

Day 1 – First the sky and earth, then the light and darkness.

Day 2 – Then waters above the sky and waters below on earth.

Day 3 – Then dry land, seas, plants, fruits, and trees with seeds.

Day 4 – Then the light and day for seasons, days, and years and the Sun for day and the Moon for night.

Day 5 – Then the waters were filled with sea animals, and the sky was filled with birds.

Day 6 – Then animals of every kind, and Human Beings to be like God – a male and a female to have many children – *only when you become an adult and get married.*

God's creation is complete. WAIT! Not yet, there is one more day . . . Whew Hoo!

Day Seven

¹So the sky, the earth and all that filled them were finished. ²By the seventh day God finished the work he had been doing. So on the seventh day he rested from all his work. ³God blessed the seventh day and made it a holy day. He made it holy because on that day he rested. He rested from all the work he had done in creating the world. (Genesis 2:1-3 ICB)

Now  God

is finished creating the World! As He told us, that on day seven, His work is done on Earth and He rested in Heaven.

Day 7 – The sky, the earth and all that filled them is finished. God rested from all His work and blessed the seventh Day and made it Holy.

Did You Know?

One more thing before we go, God has an enemy, that you need to know. Oh no! That means he is an enemy of ours also. His name is Lucifer. Just a short story, it won't take long. Don't you worry! The Bible tells us that Lucifer was the most beautiful Angel among all the other ones. (Ezekiel 28:13-15) God made him smart and wise. He put Lucifer on the Holy Mountain with the power to do great things. Then one day, Lucifer used his power to do bad things. That did not make God happy, so Lucifer had to find another home.

I'm falling

God is good and loves us all very much. He loves EVERYONE in this whole World. He wants us to love each other, share with each other, and pray for one another. You are not here by mistake; God sees everything and loves everything He creates.

Who created you?
God did!

- *Where did you come from?* **God created you from the dust in the ground!**

⁷ *Then the Lord god took dust from the ground and formed man from it. The Lord breathed the breath of life into the man's nose. And the man became a living person. (Genesis 2:7 ICB)*

- **Why are you here?**

Because God wants a Family to love and call ALL of us His own.

About the Author

Gwendolyn (Gwen) was born and raised in Madison, Indiana, where she currently resides. She was blessed with two God-fearing children that are married and have two children each of their own. She was a church treasurer for eight years at Ebenezer United Methodist Church, Madison, Indiana, where she grew up in and raised her children there as well. While at Ebenezer, she taught Sunday School for ten years, organized and implemented many children's programs within the church and educated the children in the Bible to understand how much God's love will make a difference in their relationships, friendships, and in their families. She is currently a member of Lakeview Church located in Indianapolis, IN, where she lived for ten years prior to returning home.

Gwen is a determined woman. She does not like to hear, "It can't be done!" She believes, "With God ALL things are possible. (Matthew 19:26 KJV)

ISBN 979-8-218-74554-7

9 798218 745547

90000>

www.ingramcontent.com/pod-product-compliance
Lightning Source LLC
Chambersburg PA
CBHW040857100426

42813CB00015B/2829